THIS OR THAT?
Quiz Book

by Emma MacLaren Henke

Illustrations by Karen Wolcott

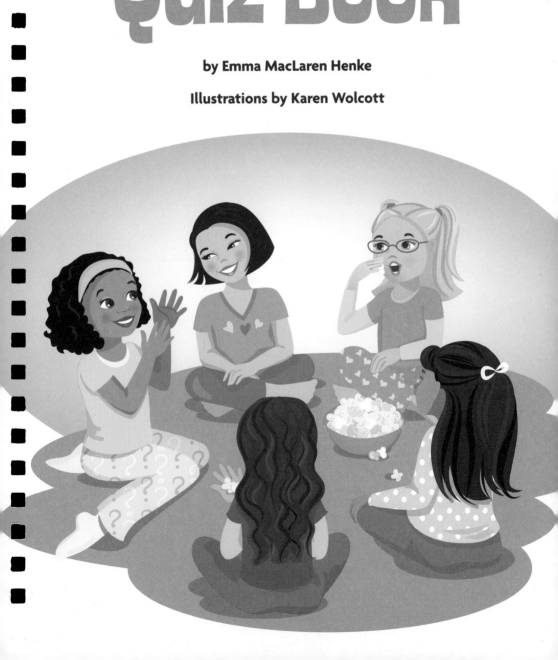

Published by American Girl Publishing

16 17 18 19 20 21 LEO 10 9 8 7 6 5 4 3 2

Editorial Development: Trula Magruder

Art Direction & Design: Lisa Wilber

Production: Tami Kepler, Sarah Boecher, Jeannette Bailey, Judith Lary

Illustrations: Karen Wolcott

The content and images in this book were not intended to represent realistic choices or activities. The book was written for entertainment purposes only. When near water, always have an adult present, and be sure to wear proper safety gear when involved in sports and other physical activities.

americangirl.com/service

Dear Reader,

Would you prefer to know more about yourself OR know more about your friends and family? We've got nearly 600 quirky questions to help you find out—the fun way!

Would you prefer to share a room with a pony OR a pot-bellied pig? The quizzes inside will help you discover all kinds of things that you didn't know about YOU.

Would you prefer to ask and answer questions with lots of friends OR just one best friend? Share the questions aloud at parties OR take a matching quiz with a friend or sibling.

Would you prefer to read all about the contents of this book OR start flipping through page after page of fun? We thought so!

Your Friends at American Girl

Table of Contents

Sleepover Survey

What makes spending the night with friends fun to you?

Would you prefer to . . .

share a sleepover with a big group **OR** one best friend?

bring along your teddy bear **OR** your favorite book?

dine on take-out pizza **OR** make your own meal?

play board games for hours **OR** have a movie marathon?

snack on popcorn **OR** snack on s'mores?

play charades **OR** have a sing-along?

tell your friends that you need a nightlight **OR** show them your favorite blankie?

sleep on the couch **OR** in a sleeping bag?

be the first one to fall asleep **OR** be the last one awake?

dream about winning
a million dollars **OR** dream about winning
a talent show?

have your friends
hear you snoring **OR** talking in
your sleep?

forget to bring
your sleeping bag **OR** forget to bring
your pajamas?

play a trick on
one of your friends **OR** be surprised by a trick
your friends play on you?

stay up late
telling secrets **OR** telling jokes?

eat an eggs-and-bacon breakfast **OR** a cereal-buffet breakfast?

spend the night
in a library **OR** at your school?

snooze in a sleeping bag
made from flower petals **OR** from a bearskin?

7

Double Dare

Do you have the nerve to choose these silly stunts?

Would you prefer to . . .

go to school wearing everything pink **OR** everything purple?

eat a whole meal without saying a word **OR** spend an entire evening without watching TV?

wear your clothes inside out for a day **OR** wear your pants tucked into your socks for a day?

perform the chicken dance for your friends **OR** sing "I'm a Little Teapot" for them?

hand in homework written in crayon **OR** call your teacher on the phone just to say hi?

spend a day talking in Pig Latin **OR** with a French or British accent?

tell a joke to your whole family **OR** to your whole class?

wear a costume to a formal party **OR** wear high-water pants to a pool party?

hand your mom a flower and tell her that it grew between your toes **OR** hand your father a paper flower and remind him to water it?

hang a sign on your bedroom door that says "I'm the boss!" **OR** hang a sign on your locker that says "I'm a genius!"?

walk into a room filled with people and yell, "[*Your Name Here*] is in the room!" **OR** dance into a room?

pretend to sneeze three times while in a car or bus **OR** snort like a pig three times?

walk up to someone you don't know at school and introduce yourself **OR** walk up to someone you *do* know and introduce yourself?

hold your finger in your ear for one minute **OR** in your nose for one minute?

let a friend style your hair **OR** let her choose your outfit?

9

Getting to Know you

Sit across from a new friend, and take this quiz together.
Share your selections to find out more about each other.

Would you prefer to . . .

have only one
pair of shoes

OR only one
pair of pants?

have one great friend

OR 20 good friends?

eat cereal
for dinner

OR a burger and fries
for breakfast?

win an acting award

OR a gold medal?

tell a knock-knock joke

OR a riddle?

give a speech in front
of your class

OR sing a song for
your whole family?

take part in a spelling bee

OR a dance marathon?

give up watching TV

OR listening to music?

take only showers
for the rest
of your life

OR only baths?

be a teacher

OR a student?

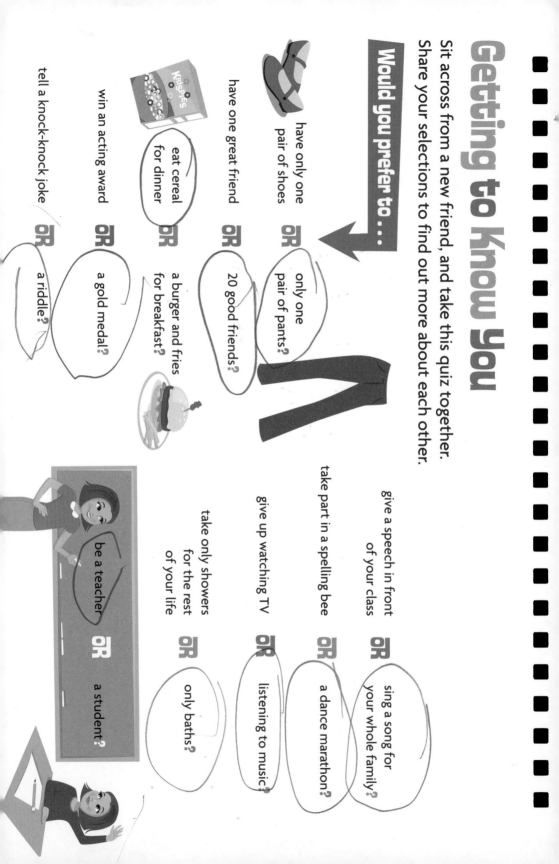

Getting to Know You

Sit across from a new friend, and take this quiz together. Share your selections to find out more about each other.

Would you prefer to . . .

have only one pair of shoes **OR** only one pair of pants?

have one great friend **OR** 20 good friends?

eat cereal for dinner **OR** a burger and fries for breakfast?

win an acting award **OR** a gold medal?

tell a knock-knock joke **OR** a riddle?

give a speech in front of your class **OR** sing a song for your whole family?

take part in a spelling bee **OR** a dance marathon?

give up watching TV **OR** listening to music?

take only showers for the rest of your life **OR** only baths?

be a teacher **OR** a student?

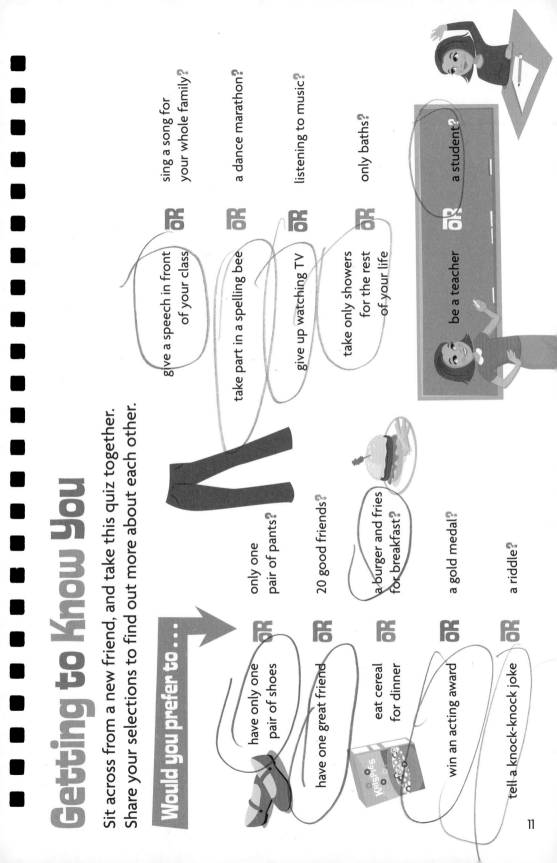

Hobby Shop

Which pastime would you pick?

Would you prefer to . . .

write your name in cross-stitch **OR** in calligraphy?

be a cliff diver **OR** a dumpster diver?

decorate a cake **OR** decorate a room?

sew a skirt **OR** knit a scarf?

learn a soccer kick **OR** a karate kick?

read a book **OR** write a poem?

play an instrument **OR** sing in a choir?

sculpt with clay **OR** build with blocks?

weave baskets **OR** shoot baskets?

dance on a stage **OR** in an exercise class?

design a dress **OR** a building?

collect stuffed animals **OR** animal fossils?

hike up a mountain **OR** ski down a mountain?

be a bird-watcher **OR** a trend watcher?

be OK at 20 different hobbies **OR** be an expert at one hobby?

paint a picture **OR** take a photograph?

plant a flower garden **OR** arrange a bouquet?

Parent Trap

How well do you know your mom and dad? Ask each one the questions below. Circle your mom's answer in pen and your dad's in pencil. Surprised?

Would you prefer to . . .

win a major football game	OR	pitch a no-hitter?
ask me to choose your outfits for a week	OR	choose your next haircut?
go without a coat all winter	OR	have to wear a coat all summer?
be the president of our country for a day	OR	the mayor of our town for a year?
never again mow your grass	OR	never wash your car?
live without a stove	OR	without a refrigerator?
go skydiving	OR	deep-sea diving?

roller-skate to work **OR** skateboard to the grocery store?

eat my favorite meal **OR** watch my favorite movie?

have to go to my school for a week **OR** have me do your job for a week?

never again shave **OR** never again wash your hair?

never again take out the garbage **OR** never do the laundry?

spend a week without your computer **OR** without your phone?

build a log cabin in Alaska **OR** a beach house in Florida?

travel the globe in a sailboat **OR** in a hot-air balloon?

spend a day as the teacher of my class **OR** the principal of my school?

Write Yourself In

What if you played a role in your favorite books and movies?

Would you prefer to . . .

solve mysteries like Nancy Drew **OR** travel around the world like Flat Stanley?

have Garfield for a pet **OR** Scooby-Doo?

take a tour of a famous chocolate factory **OR** take a journey inside a giant peach?

wake up to find yourself with Dorothy in the land of Oz **OR** with Alice down the rabbit hole?

be the hero of an action movie **OR** a romantic comedy?

live in a tree house with the Swiss Family Robinson **OR** on a pirate ship with Long John Silver?

run away to live at an art museum **OR** in an abandoned boxcar?

have a best friend who's an elf **OR** a hobbit?

ride the Black Stallion **OR** have Lassie for a pet?

kiss an ogre **OR** a frog-prince?

live under the sea with Nemo **OR** the Little Mermaid?

discover a secret garden **OR** a wardrobe that's a passage to a magical world?

have a magical nanny like Mary Poppins **OR** a singing nanny like Maria from *The Sound of Music*?

eat fried worms **OR** get the "cheese touch"?

spend a day in Neverland with the Lost Boys **OR** in the jungle with Mowgli?

Road Trip!

Bored in the car? See how your seatmates answer these questions.

Would you prefer to . . .

sightsee from the front seat **OR** read a book in the backseat?

drive through the mountains **OR** along the coast?

travel across the country in a semi **OR** a school bus?

stop for burgers **OR** a picnic?

drive 12 hours straight **OR** make a stop every hour?

snack on candy **OR** pretzels?

pass the time singing songs **OR** playing word games?

ride in a car with no radio **OR** no air-conditioning?

share the backseat with your next-door neighbor **OR** your teacher?

Would you rather...

share a car with 100 kittens **OR** 15 dogs?

ride in a car driving 30 miles per hour **OR** 1,000 miles per hour?

follow a road map **OR** flip a coin to decide directions?

travel the whole day without stopping for food **OR** without stopping for a bathroom break?

drive on a gravel road **OR** in a traffic jam?

stop at every historical marker you pass **OR** every scenic overlook?

get up with the sun, and start traveling early **OR** sleep in late, and drive into the night?

stay in a motel **OR** travel with a camper?

Family Tree

How far would you branch out?

Would you prefer to . . .

be the oldest child in your family **OR** the youngest?

dress in the clothes your mom wore when she was your age **OR** in the clothes your great-grandmother wore?

spend a day in the life of your mom's childhood **OR** your dad's childhood?

discover you're descended from a famous ruler **OR** a famous writer?

have all your relatives living in the same town **OR** have relatives all over the world?

discover you have a cousin who looks just like you **OR** who was born on the same day as you?

have another older sibling **OR** another younger sibling?

learn about your family history on your mom's side **OR** your dad's side?

be an only child **OR** have ten siblings?

babysit for younger siblings **OR** have older siblings babysit for you?

be related to a movie star **OR** a famous athlete?

inherit a piece of jewelry **OR** a work of art?

go to a family reunion with 300 guests **OR** a family party with your ten closest relatives?

meet your great-great-great-grandmother **OR** your great-great-great-granddaughter?

share a family dinner with your coach **OR** your teacher?

wear hand-me-down clothes **OR** use a hand-me-down bike?

have your family's embarrassing movie on a funny home-videos TV show **OR** have your mom show your class your naked baby pictures?

Style File

Discover your fashion passion.

Would you prefer to . . .

wear polka dots **OR** stripes?

dress in only one color **OR** in clashing colors?

wear socks with toes **OR** fingerless gloves?

hit the beach in a one-piece **OR** a bikini?

wear sandals every day **OR** tennis shoes?

always wear skirts **OR** always wear pants?

have long hair you can wear only in a ponytail	**OR**	shorter hair you can wear however you like?
wear socks with sandals	**OR**	pants that are too short?
wear a dress made from duct tape	**OR**	a hat made from newspaper?
decorate your clothes with flowers	**OR**	rhinestones?
always wear your shirt tucked in	**OR**	always leave your shirt untucked?
make all your own clothes	**OR**	buy all your clothes at a thrift store?
always wear tank tops	**OR**	always wear long sleeves?

stay warm with a warm-up jacket	**OR**	a peacoat?
wear a shirt with a hole in it	**OR**	with a stain on it?
choose outfits for your best friend to wear	**OR**	let her choose outfits for you?
wear rainbow suspenders	**OR**	rainbow kneesocks?

Playtime!

Are you game for this quiz?

Would you prefer to . . .

play chess with life-size pieces **OR** play "Go Fish" with real fish?

learn a yo-yo trick **OR** a card trick?

sail a remote-controlled boat on a pond **OR** fly a remote-controlled helicopter in a field?

master the game of jacks **OR** pick-up sticks?

get to school on stilts **OR** a pogo stick?

live in a dollhouse **OR** a bouncy house?

have a huge collection of stuffed animals **OR** trading cards?

24

play shuffleboard
with pancakes **OR** play Ping-Pong
with grapes**?**

cook a meal
in a toy kitchen **OR** build a doghouse
with toy tools**?**

give up computer games **OR** board games**?**

catch water-balloons **OR** make balloon animals**?**

kick a soccer ball **OR** hit a tennis ball**?**

play checkers **OR** dominoes**?**

be in a water-balloon fight **OR** a snowball fight**?**

always travel on your bike **OR** on roller skates**?**

invent a new video game **OR** a new board game**?**

build a house of cards **OR** a pillow fort**?**

25

Wiggle Room

What does your space say about you?

Would you prefer to . . .

have furniture made from marshmallows **OR** colorful hard candy?

have to make your bed every day for the rest of your life **OR** never sleep in a made bed again?

paint your room all black **OR** all hot pink?

have a pillowcase with a horse **OR** hearts?

share a room with a sibling **OR** with a parent?

sleep with your stuffed animals **OR** your pet?

have a computer in your room **OR** a phone?

have an alarm clock that wakes you by telling jokes **OR** by squirting you with water?

Knock, knock . . .

7:15

hang up a disco ball **OR** a dream catcher?

sleep on the top bunk of a triple-decker bunk bed **OR** on a mattress on the floor?

have a room made entirely of windows **OR** a room with no windows at all?

put up posters of your favorite musician **OR** your favorite athlete?

have a room on the top floor of your house **OR** in the basement?

spend time in your room reading **OR** playing with your toys?

have a room with a built-in bathroom **OR** a walk-in closet?

clean your room every day **OR** clean your room once a year?

sleep without a pillow **OR** without a blanket?

27

Friendship Flip

Sit across from a friend, and take this quiz to see if you're two peas in a pod or opposites who attract.

Would you prefer to . . .

give your friend a gift of jewelry **OR** a book?

get together with your friend every day for a month **OR** every weekend for a year?

see your friend only at school **OR** only out of school?

communicate with your friend only through notes **OR** text message?

share a bedroom with your friend **OR** always be in the same class as your friend?

invite your friend on your family vacation **OR** to your summer camp?

share your friend's wardrobe **OR** her toys?

share one chocolate ice cream cone **OR** each have your own vanilla milk shake?

share a secret language **OR** share a secret about someone you both know?

trade places with your friend on a school day **OR** on a weekend?

Hi Kate!

CU SOON

28

Friendship Flip

Sit across from a friend, and take this quiz to see
if you're two peas in a pod or opposites who attract.

Would you prefer to . . . . .

give your friend
a gift of jewelry

OR

a book?

get together with
your friend every
day for a month

OR

every weekend
for a year?

see your friend
only at school

OR

only out of school?

communicate with
your friend only
through notes

OR

text messages?

share a bedroom
with your friend

OR

always be in the same
class as your friend?

invite your friend on
your family vacation

OR

to your summer camp?

share your
friend's wardrobe

OR

her toys?

share one
chocolate
ice cream cone

OR

each have
your own
vanilla milk shake?

share a secret language

OR

share a secret about
someone you both know?

trade places
with your friend
on a school day

OR

on a weekend?

Sticky Situations

How do you handle the "oops" in your life?

Would you prefer to . . .

split your pants
when you bend over

OR

trip over your flip-flops?

unintentionally invite your
entire class to a party

OR

have the entire class hear
you only invite one person?

forget to send
a thank-you
note for a gift

OR

forget to bring
a gift to a
birthday party?

go to detention
at school

OR

get grounded
at home?

tell a lie to
your best friend

OR

find out that
she lied to you?

forget your
friend's birthday

OR

forget your
parent's birthday?

burp out loud in front
of your grandmother

OR

your teacher?

get caught talking
with your mouth full

OR

chewing with
your mouth open?

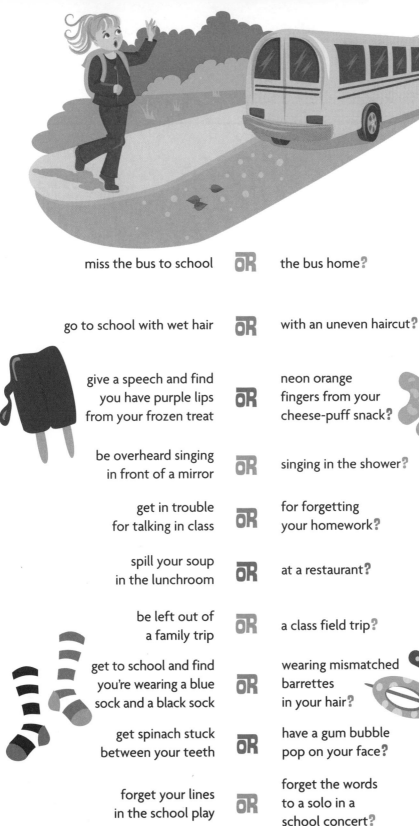

miss the bus to school **OR** the bus home?

go to school with wet hair **OR** with an uneven haircut?

give a speech and find you have purple lips from your frozen treat **OR** neon orange fingers from your cheese-puff snack?

be overheard singing in front of a mirror **OR** singing in the shower?

get in trouble for talking in class **OR** for forgetting your homework?

spill your soup in the lunchroom **OR** at a restaurant?

be left out of a family trip **OR** a class field trip?

get to school and find you're wearing a blue sock and a black sock **OR** wearing mismatched barrettes in your hair?

get spinach stuck between your teeth **OR** have a gum bubble pop on your face?

forget your lines in the school play **OR** forget the words to a solo in a school concert?

31

Mirror, Mirror

A crazy wizard takes over your life. What now?

Would you prefer that the wizard flicks a wand and . . .

makes roses grow between your toes	**OR**	daisies grow on top of your head?
gives you a bushy beard	**OR**	a hairy back?
removes all the anger you'll ever feel	**OR**	all the hurt feelings?
makes you grow a squirrel's tail	**OR**	bunny ears?
turns your lips bright orange	**OR**	your eyes bright red?
creates a twin sister for you	**OR**	a twin brother?
the sun turns red	**OR**	the moon turns green?
makes your teacher call you Sock Monkey	**OR**	Huggy Bear?
forces you to walk backward all day	**OR**	on your knees?

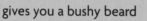

makes you wear a sock
puppet on your hand all day **OR** a pirate eye patch?

turns you
into a dog **OR** a cat?

it rains every
time you laugh **OR** people around
you laugh
every time you cry?

forces you to
dress in a different
outfit every hour **OR** wear the same
outfit for a week?

makes you
wear a hat
covered in feathers **OR** a hat covered
in pom-poms?

turns your hair purple **OR** your teeth gold?

gives you permanent
silver eye shadow **OR** silver nail polish?

it never gets dark **OR** it never gets cold?

freezes your hand into
a permanent peace sign **OR** a permanent thumbs-up?

Talk to the Animals

Take a walk on the wild side.

Would you prefer to . . .

understand bird tweets **OR** dolphin squeaks?

run as fast as a cheetah **OR** swim like a shark?

detect scents like an elephant **OR** leave a trail of slime like a snail?

float like a butterfly **OR** sting like a bee?

be covered in fur like a bear **OR** in scales like a snake?

eat only lettuce and carrots like a hamster **OR** only meat like a cat?

have a tail like a monkey's **OR** a nose like a bloodhound's?

stay awake all night with the owls **OR** wake at the crack of dawn with the roosters?

live at the bottom of the ocean **OR** atop rainforest trees?

glow like a
lightning bug **OR** have feathers
like a peacock's?

gallop like a horse **OR** climb like a mountain goat?

eat dog biscuits **OR** fish food?

live in a beaver dam **OR** in a bird's nest?

fly south for the winter **OR** hibernate through it?

see in the dark like a cat **OR** hear as well as a dog?

talk in oinks **OR** moos?

live in a zoo **OR** at a pet store?

jump like a frog **OR** slither like a snake?

have fleas **OR** shed your skin?

have a pouch
like a kangaroo's **OR** a shell
like a turtle's?

Pick a Pet

Which furry friend would make you smile?

Would you prefer to . . .

have a huge fish tank filled with plain goldfish **OR** a small fishbowl with one exotic fish?

own a mouse that can dance **OR** a cat that can jump rope?

take swimming lessons with a seal **OR** ride a zebra to school?

pet an armadillo **OR** a porcupine?

take care of a dog that never needs to be walked **OR** never needs to be fed?

let a pet tarantula crawl up your arm **OR** a pet snake wrap around your waist?

own a dog big enough to ride **OR** a horse small enough to walk on a leash?

share your room
with a miniature pony **OR** a potbellied pig?

bring a bunny to
school every day **OR** a ferret?

hear an owl hooting outside
your window every night **OR** a rooster crowing
every morning?

drink from your
cat's water bowl **OR** take a bath
with your dog?

have a goat that climbs on top
of your bed every morning **OR** a goat that loves to
eat your shoes?

brush and groom
a Persian cat **OR** trim and primp
a poodle?

live with a
pet elephant **OR** a pet whale?

own a different
pet every year **OR** the same pet
your whole life?

keep a pygmy hippo
for a classroom pet **OR** a reindeer?

own a pet rock **OR** a virtual pet?

Wild Work

Check out these career choices in the animal kingdom.

Would you prefer to . . .

be a vet for family pets **OR** farm animals?

milk cows **OR** rope bulls?

photograph rare birds **OR** film sharks attacking their prey?

train police dogs **OR** train dogs to perform on TV?

trim poodles as a dog groomer **OR** shear sheep as a wool farmer?

wear an animal mascot costume **OR** be the voice of a cartoon animal?

run a pet store **OR** an animal shelter?

perform with dolphins at a water park **OR** with lions in a circus act?

raise a new
breed of dog **OR** study a new
breed of insect?

ride a racehorse **OR** change a horse's shoes
and brush its mane?

clean fish tanks at a
marine sanctuary **OR** elephant cages at a zoo?

take care of baby
gorillas at a zoo **OR** study gorillas in a jungle?

walk dogs **OR** judge dog shows?

get rich running your
own pet-sitting business **OR** your own pet
clothing business?

work as a beekeeper **OR** a snake charmer?

get a job
as a zookeeper **OR** as an animal ranger
at a nature park?

lead safaris
in Africa **OR** guide guests
through the arctic
to spot polar bears?

Sweet Tooth

Candies and cookies and cakes—oh my!

Would you prefer to . . .

eat only milk chocolate **OR** white chocolate?

eat one great homemade chocolate chip cookie **OR** ten store-bought ones?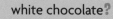

lick an everlasting ice cream cone **OR** drink a bottomless milk shake?

swim in a chocolate river **OR** float on a cotton-candy cloud?

try spinach ice cream **OR** bacon cookies?

eat one jelly bean every day for a year **OR** 365 jelly beans at once only one time a year?

give up Halloween candy **OR** birthday cakes?

invent a best-selling candy bar **OR** create a prize-winning cake recipe?

40

eat the same
dessert every day **OR** try a new dessert
once a week?

work in an
ice cream factory **OR** a bakery?

eat a tablespoon
of plain sugar **OR** unsweetened cocoa?

snack on chocolate-
covered pretzels **OR** chocolate-covered
raisins?

live in a
gingerbread house **OR** a candy house?

savor one gourmet
chocolate by yourself **OR** share a plate of cookies
with your friends?

eat a life-sized
marshmallow bird **OR** a life-sized
chocolate bunny?

eat a dozen donuts **OR** a whole pie?

eat cake
without frosting **OR** frosting
without cake?

41

Tongue Twisters

These crazy flavors would test your taste buds.

Would you prefer to . . .

drink a meatloaf milk shake	OR	eat a smoothie-flavored sandwich?
eat a hamburger on a hot dog bun	OR	a hot dog on a hamburger bun?
eat a frozen pizza on a stick	OR	bacon-flavored ice cream?
give up milk on your cereal	OR	ketchup on your fries?
have Thanksgiving turkey stuffed with marshmallows	OR	chocolate pie topped with gravy?
give up salty snacks	OR	desserts?
down a dish of hot ice cream	OR	cold soup?
eat salsa on a hamburger	OR	ketchup on a taco?
smell delicious bread baking without eating it	OR	eat bread without tasting it?
chew gum flavored like garlic	OR	like a pickle?

eat chili on the hottest day of the year **OR** ice cream on the coldest day?

take one bite of a food you hate **OR** eat a full meal of food you've never tried?

eat only breakfast foods for a week **OR** only dinner foods?

eat a meal wearing a blindfold **OR** wearing nose plugs?

 try fried grasshoppers **OR** chocolate-covered ants?

eat spaghetti with a spoon **OR** soup with a fork?

salt your ice cream **OR** put hot fudge on your popcorn?

eat purple mac and cheese **OR** green peanut butter?

 eat marshmallow fluff and peanut butter **OR** chocolate and peanut butter?

try alligator on a stick from Louisiana **OR** fried rattlesnake from Texas?

eat a sandwich with no bread **OR** a taco with no shell?

Super Powers

Choose the skills that could help you save the world.

Would you prefer to . . .

shrink to the size of a flea **OR** grow to 100 feet tall?

run faster than a speeding bullet **OR** leap tall buildings in a single bound?

fly **OR** be invisible?

have X-ray vision **OR** supersonic hearing?

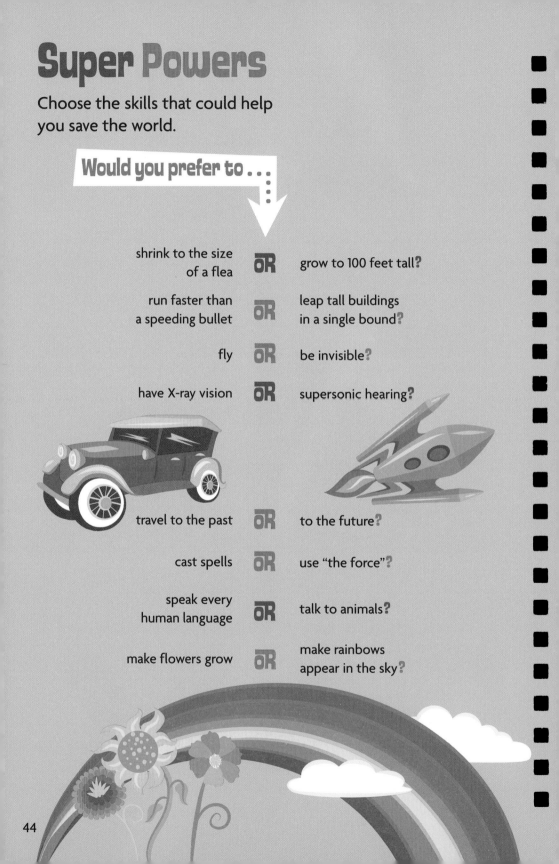

travel to the past **OR** to the future?

cast spells **OR** use "the force"?

speak every human language **OR** talk to animals?

make flowers grow **OR** make rainbows appear in the sky?

breathe in
outer space **OR** breathe
underwater?

see in the dark **OR** see things
far, far away?

be a werewolf **OR** a vampire?

control electricity **OR** gravity?

control the weather **OR** change the length
of day and night?

have a super memory **OR** be super sensitive
to how others feel?

squeeze through any size hole **OR** turn to sand and blow
through any hole?

know whenever
others are lying **OR** know whenever
they're afraid?

have hair that
turns into fingers **OR** skin that changes
into steel?

control other
people's thoughts **OR** their actions?

Shopping Spree

What would you buy with unlimited cash?

Would you prefer to . . .

live in a mansion **OR** a fancy hotel?

spend all your money on one big thing **OR** spend it on lots and lots of little things?

treat your friends to the best shopping spree ever **OR** buy a new wardrobe of designer duds for yourself?

add a waterslide to your home **OR** build a baseball diamond in your yard?

buy season tickets for life for your favorite sports team **OR** for your city's symphony?

drive an expensive sports car **OR** hire a limousine and driver?

eat at fancy restaurants as often as you like **OR** treat all your friends to pizza lunch for the rest of your days in school?

start your own business **OR** fund extracurricular activities for your whole school?

buy a million dollars worth of shoes and clothes **OR** a million dollars worth of sports equipment?

spend a month living in Buckingham Palace **OR** in the White House?

donate your money to help cure a disease **OR** to help save an endangered animal?

pay for a pet panda bear **OR** a monkey trained to be your butler?

buy a narrow swimming pool that winds through your house **OR** a large pool that takes up most of your large bedroom?

hire a fashion designer who chooses amazing outfits each day **OR** a chef who prepares whatever you feel like eating?

fly around the world in first class **OR** cruise around the world on a luxury boat?

buy a chocolate factory **OR** a jelly-bean factory?

pay for a private concert by your favorite singer **OR** spend a month touring with your favorite singer?

buy a seat on a space flight to the moon **OR** spend a month in a submarine exploring the ocean?

Sibling Rivalry

Face off with your brother or sister to take this quiz.
Then compare answers to see how you stack up.

Would you prefer to . . .

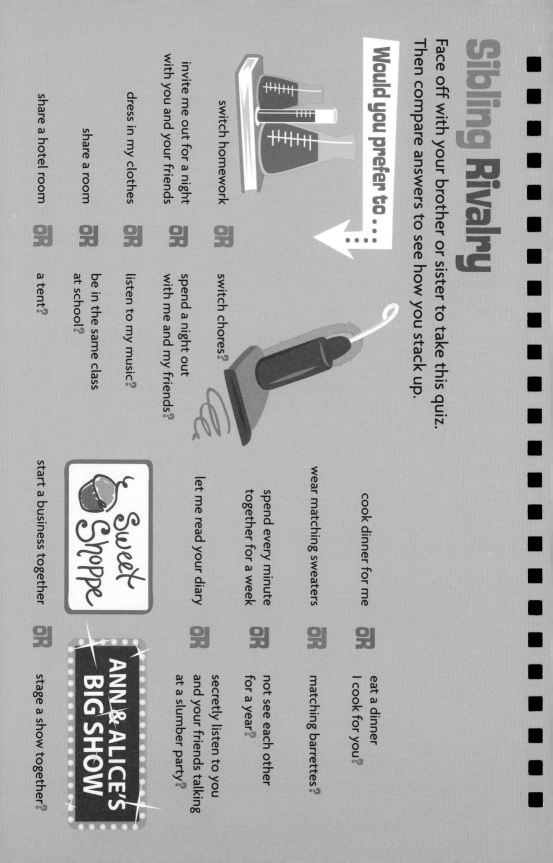

switch homework **OR** switch chores?

cook dinner for me	**OR**	eat a dinner I cook for you?

wear matching sweaters **OR** matching barrettes?

invite me out for a night with you and your friends **OR** spend a night out with me and my friends?

spend every minute together for a week **OR** not see each other for a year?

dress in my clothes **OR** listen to my music?

let me read your diary **OR** secretly listen to you and your friends talking at a slumber party?

share a room **OR** be in the same class at school?

share a hotel room **OR** a tent?

start a business together **OR** stage a show together?

Sweet Shoppe

ANN & ALICE'S BIG SHOW

sprinkle your friends with fairy dust **OR** make them grow fairy wings?

cook every meal in a witch's cauldron **OR** always wear a wizard's hat?

use magic to make people laugh **OR** to make them cry?

taste a potion made from eye of newt **OR** from toe of frog?

ride a winged horse **OR** a broomstick?

have a magic candle that lights whenever you need it **OR** have the power to make a room instantly dark?

know a great card trick **OR** be able to pull a rabbit from a hat?

tell your friends' futures with a crystal ball **OR** see your own future there?

A Lot to Learn

Discover your school style.

Would you prefer to . . .

get an A on your
science-fair project **OR** your art project?

eat three meals a day
in the school cafeteria **OR** go without eating
while you're at school?

clean a messy locker **OR** wash stinky gym clothes?

wear your school
colors every day **OR** always wear black and white?

go to an all-girls' school **OR** a coed school?

memorize 100 spelling words **OR** solve 100 math problems?

do homework at 4 PM **OR** at 8 PM?

never have to
do homework again **OR** never have to
take another test?

Would you rather...

forget to study for a test **OR** forget to do your homework?

know all the answers on a history test **OR** place first on a fitness test?

teach your English class **OR** your music class?

be the president of the student council **OR** the star of the school play?

go to a school without computers **OR** one without a library?

serve lunch in the cafeteria **OR** clean up the teachers' lounge?

do your homework on a chalkboard **OR** a dry-erase board?

chew old gum you find inside your desk **OR** eat the cafeteria's "mystery meat"?

live without pencils **OR** pens?

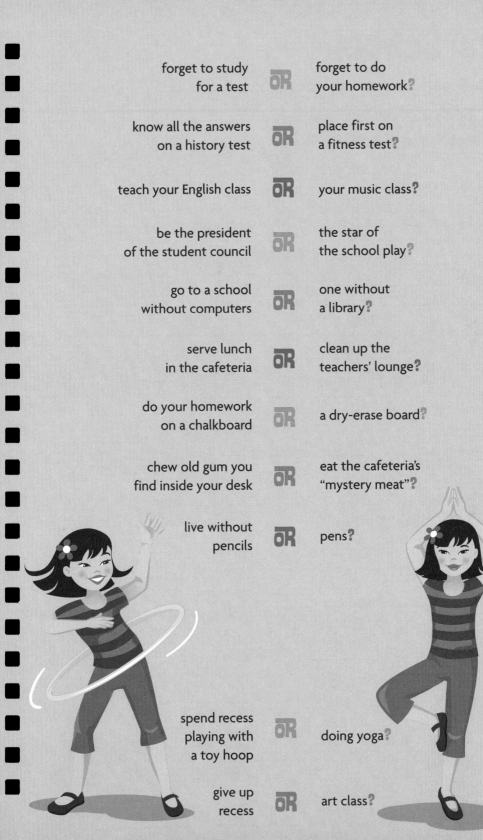

spend recess playing with a toy hoop **OR** doing yoga?

give up recess **OR** art class?

Silly School

Laughter and learning can go hand in hand!

Would you prefer to . . .

take social studies
in the school pool **OR** music on top
of the jungle gym**?**

go to school
in your pajamas **OR** in your
bathing suit**?**

make a movie for
a school project **OR** a music video**?**

take an animal-
training class **OR** a dance class**?**

take a class
in craft projects **OR** board-game playing**?**

have only one pencil
for the class to share **OR** one desk**?**

have your parents as classmates **OR** as teachers?

eat picnic lunches **OR** fancy dining lunches?

have your school mascot be Santa Claus **OR** the Tooth Fairy?

take all your classes at a clown college **OR** a rodeo college?

take art class while doing yoga poses **OR** take gym class in high heels?

roller-skate to school **OR** swim to school?

attend a school for witches and wizards **OR** a school for superheroes?

go to school all summer long **OR** every Saturday?

wear school uniforms that look like fairy and elf outfits **OR** futuristic space suits?

Making History

What if you could travel back in time?

Would you prefer to . . .

see a
dodo bird **OR** a woolly
mammoth?

be a pilgrim on
the *Mayflower* **OR** a Native American
greeting the pilgrims?

use the first telephone **OR** watch the first movie?

discover the Grand Canyon **OR** Old Faithful?

live in ancient Egypt **OR** ancient Greece?

wear a
hoop skirt **OR** a flapper dress?

see gladiators battle
in Rome's Coliseum **OR** see Shakespeare act in
one of his plays in London?

churn your own butter **OR** bake your own bread?

travel across the West
in a covered wagon **OR** on the first
cross-country train?

watch the first
airplane flight **OR** the first
moon landing?

learn how to make
your own pottery **OR** weave your
own cloth?

quit school to work
on the family farm **OR** take care of your siblings?

make your home
in a castle **OR** on a pirate ship?

take a bath
in a washtub **OR** go to the bathroom
in an outhouse?

meet the country's founders **OR** your own ancestors?

brush your teeth with a twig **OR** use the same bathwater
as the rest of your family?

live in a
log cabin **OR** a tepee?

57

Fast Forward

What will your life be like in 25 years?

Would you prefer to . . .

have ten children **OR** none at all?

be married to someone you know now **OR** to someone you haven't yet met?

be a fabulous cook **OR** eat most of your meals at restaurants?

work for a big company **OR** work for yourself?

have hair that is completely gray **OR** still have pimples?

dress like a movie star **OR** dress like a famous athlete?

have the same friends you have now **OR** have a new set of friends?

work from home
every day

OR

have a job that lets
you travel the world?

live in the
same state
you live in now

OR

live in a
different
country?

live in a high-rise
apartment

OR

a country
farmhouse?

live next door
to your parents

OR

live in a different
state from them?

live in the middle
of a huge city

OR

live 100 miles away from
your closest neighbor?

live by yourself

OR

live with your big family?

hold the world record
for the longest hair

OR

the longest fingernails?

take a vacation
camping in Alaska

OR

touring the art
museums of Paris?

What's Your Dream Job?

What do you think is the coolest career?

Would you prefer to . . .

be a Supreme Court justice **OR** a judge on a TV talent contest?

star in a movie **OR** write a movie script?

taste-test candy **OR** design new toys?

be president of a very cool and exciting company **OR** President of the United States?

be a fashion model **OR** a fashion photographer?

test new video games **OR** review new movies?

be the head chef
at a fancy restaurant **OR** own a cupcake bakery?

discover a cure for
a terrible disease **OR** discover a way to
make humans fly?

create paintings sold
at art galleries **OR** design skyscrapers for
the world's biggest cities?

star in a Broadway show **OR** study the stars in space?

write popular mystery novels **OR** solve real-life mysteries?

live with gorillas in the
mountains of Africa **OR** study giant squid
under the sea?

buy shoes for
department stores **OR** design shoes for
performance shows?

appear in a TV sitcom **OR** on a TV reality show?

build designer
doghouses **OR** invent an automatic
pooper-scooper?

Get Rich Quick

Just how far would you go to get one million dollars?

Would you prefer to . . .

give up talking
on the phone **OR** give up watching
television?

lose the ability
to laugh **OR** to tell a lie?

spend a year
living in a submarine **OR** a hot-air balloon?

spend a year
in roller skates **OR** a year walking on stilts
everywhere you go?

never eat meat again **OR** never eat candy again?

always talk in
a silly accent **OR** always shout
when you talk?

Would you rather...

wear a potato sack as your wedding dress **OR** make your own clothes for the rest of your life?

have to tickle every new person you meet **OR** have to tell every person you meet your most embarrassing moment?

have a Komodo dragon as a pet **OR** live in a house with 100 cats?

let your biggest enemy choose the house where you will live **OR** the food that you will eat?

always wear clown makeup **OR** always wear clown shoes?

let TV cameras film everything you do **OR** reveal your family's secrets on a talk show?

judge a contest for the worst-smelling thing in the world **OR** not take a shower or bath for a year?

move your family to Antarctica **OR** to the Amazon rainforest?

Friends Forever?

Take this quiz with a pal to find out how your choices stand the test of time.

Would you prefer to . . . ?

go to the same college
as your friend
OR
live in the same town
after college?

have your friend
babysit your children
OR
have your friend be
part of your wedding?

change your names
to Lucy and Ethel
OR
Alex and Harper?

take your friend on a
vacation on the world's
most luxurious yacht
OR
to the world's
most luxurious
resort?

celebrate only
your 100th
birthday together
OR
celebrate every
birthday together
for the next 20 years?

be stranded on
a desert island with
your friend for a year
OR
never be able
to spend any time
alone with her again?

live in different countries
OR
live next door to
each other forever?

write a book
together
OR
run a bookstore
together?

become a famous
singing duo
OR
a famous
comedy team?

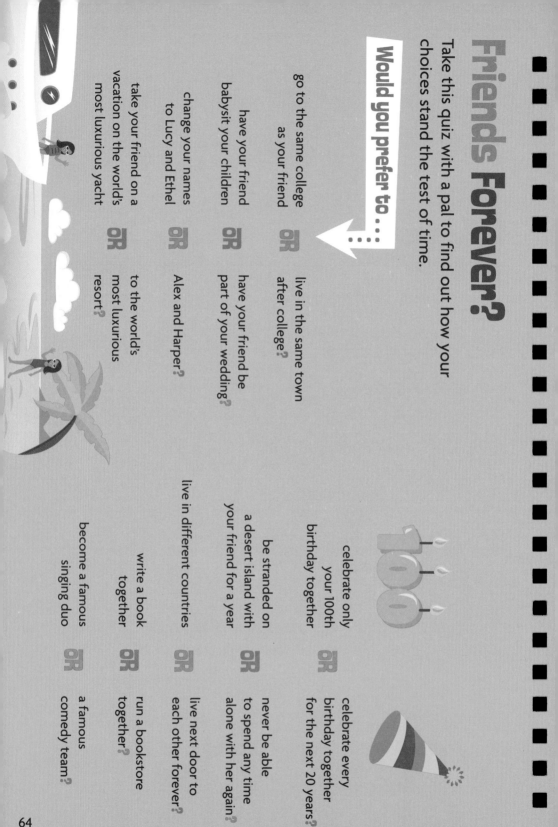

Friends Forever?

Take this quiz with a pal to find out how your choices stand the test of time.

Would you prefer to . . . :

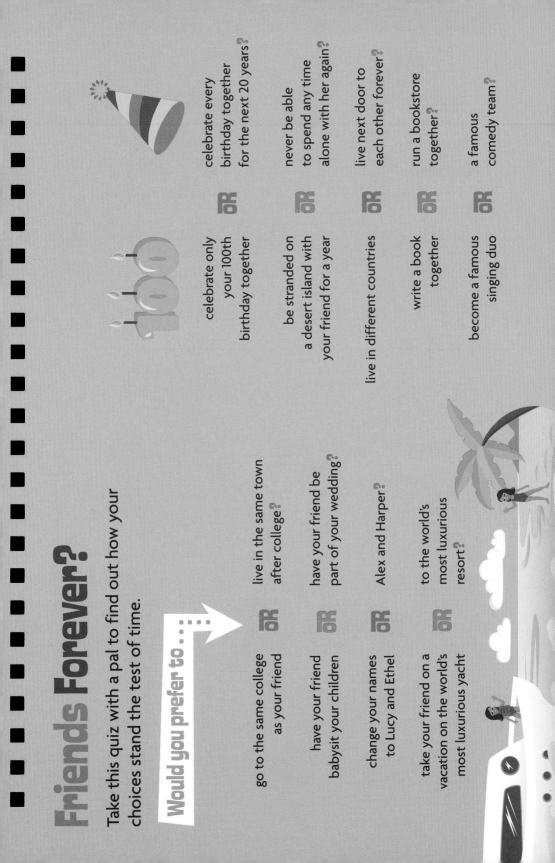

go to the same college
as your friend

OR

live in the same town
after college?

have your friend
babysit your children

OR

have your friend be
part of your wedding?

change your names
to Lucy and Ethel

OR

Alex and Harper?

take your friend on a
vacation on the world's
most luxurious yacht

OR

to the world's
most luxurious
resort?

celebrate only
your 100th
birthday together

OR

celebrate every
birthday together
for the next 20 years?

be stranded on
a desert island with
your friend for a year

OR

never be able
to spend any time
alone with her again?

live in different countries

OR

live next door to
each other forever?

write a book
together

OR

run a bookstore
together?

become a famous
singing duo

OR

a famous
comedy team?

Space Age

What will life be like 100 years from now?
Or 1,000 years from now?

Would you prefer to . . .

step into a teleporter and arrive
at your friend's house instantly **OR** travel there in a mini helicopter
from your rooftop?

take a high-speed
elevator to the moon **OR** fly your own
rocket?

travel in time **OR** live to be 1,000 years old?

have a house full
of furniture made
from recycled paper **OR** wear clothes made
from recycled plastic?

live in an era without cars **OR** without garbage?

take "food pills"
instead of eating **OR** take "brain pills"
instead of reading?

live on a space station **OR** in a plastic bubble on earth?

drive a flying car **OR** wear a jet pack?

have a robot friend **OR** a robot pet?

have wall paintings that speak with you as you walk by **OR** be able to tell your appliances what you want them to do?

power your car with water **OR** with cut grass?

own a pet that never ages **OR** have a sibling who never ages?

live in a world where all people speak the same language **OR** where all people know every language?

be able to talk to animals **OR** be able to move objects with your mind?

own a bicycle that rides on land and water **OR** or rides up walls?

World Traveler

Take a look at these tempting vacations.

Would you prefer to . . .

bike across the country **OR** cruise around the world?

spend a night in The Plaza Hotel in New York **OR** sleep under the stars on safari in Africa?

spend Cinco de Mayo in Mexico City **OR** a Chinese New Year in Beijing?

bird-watch in the Amazon **OR** people-watch in Tokyo?

climb the stairs to the top of the world's tallest building **OR** hike up the world's tallest mountain?

taste a plate of pâté in Paris **OR** a bowl of borscht in Moscow?

see the "Mona Lisa" **OR** the Taj Mahal?

have your face on Mount Rushmore **OR** as the new Statue of Liberty?

ride a barrel safely over Niagara Falls **OR** take a bath with snow monkeys in the hot springs of Japan?

stay in a hut on
a tropical island with
one friend for two weeks

OR

with two friends
for one week?

spend a night
in King Tut's Tomb

OR

in a jail cell
at Alcatraz?

spend the night
in an amusement-park
haunted house with friends

OR

spend a week on an
amusement-park boat ride?

dress in furs
with the Inuit

OR

wear a grass skirt
in Hawaii?

stay up to see the
midnight sun in Alaska

OR

visit the penguins
in Antarctica?

take a ride on
a cheetah's back

OR

in a kangaroo's pouch?

row a boat across
the English Channel

OR

swim across
the Mississippi River?

Be a Sport

Find your inner athlete with this quiz!

Would you prefer to . . .

referee a soccer game **OR** judge a gymnastics meet?

run a marathon **OR** hike up a mountain?

glide across the ice
as a figure skater **OR** glide across the stage
as a dancer?

compete against
Serena Williams in tennis **OR** Shawn Johnson
in gymnastics?

master yoga **OR** karate?

go white-water
rafting **OR** sail a boat on
the open seas?

jump out of
an airplane **OR** dive off a cliff?

bounce over
moguls on snow skis **OR** bounce over
waves on water skis?

do a flip off
the diving board **OR** the balance beam**?**

work out at a
rock-climbing gym **OR** a boxing club**?**

bike up a mountain
at your own pace **OR** bike down a mountain
as fast as possible**?**

learn how to do
a trick on a snowboard **OR** a surfboard**?**

bowl a
perfect game **OR** be the goalie in
a shutout victory**?**

swim a mile
in the ocean **OR** run ten miles
on the beach**?**

try bungee jumping **OR** hang gliding**?**

hit a baseball
over the fence **OR** hit a hole-in-one
on a golf course**?**

skate across your state **OR** in circles on a Roller Derby team**?**

box against your best friend **OR** arm-wrestle your mom**?**

go spelunking in a cave **OR** scuba diving in the sea**?**

71

Truth or Truth?

Share this twist on the classic party game with your pals!

Would you prefer to . . .

describe your most
embarrassing moment
OR
the strangest dream
you ever had?

reveal the worst
grade you ever got
OR
the time you got into
the most trouble
with your parents?

tell what you love
the most about yourself
OR
what you love the least?

tell what you'd like to ask
for as a birthday gift
OR
what you wished for when
you blew out the candles on
your last birthday cake?

describe how your family
celebrates the holidays
OR
tell a funny story from
your family vacation?

tell the one thing you think
you're worst at and why
OR
tell about a secret
talent you have?

reveal who you think
makes a great friend and why
OR
what you'd like to do
to be an even better friend?

explain what you're
most grateful for
OR
the memory that makes
you the happiest?

tell the group
your secret fear
OR
tell about a time
something silly
really frightened you?

tell where you are ticklish	**OR**	describe something silly that always makes you laugh?
tell who you think is the most beautiful or handsome person you know	**OR**	reveal your celebrity crush?
reveal what you'd most like to change about the world	**OR**	a piece of advice you'd most like to give someone?
tell about your favorite day this week and why	**OR**	your favorite teacher and why?
reveal the most money you've ever saved	**OR**	the worst thing you've ever bought with your own money?

Quiz Calendar

Enjoy quick questions for the special days of the year.

On New Year's Day, would you prefer to . . .

spend the whole day
sleeping in

OR

never go to
bed at all?

go to the Tournament
of Roses parade

OR

the Rose Bowl
football game?

Sing "Auld Lang Syne"
over and over for an hour

OR

watch a crystal ball that
takes an hour to drop?

For Groundhog Day, would you prefer to . . .

wait six weeks for sunny
spring weather

OR

have an early—but
rainy—spring?

be bound by the
groundhog's prediction

OR

be sure that he can't
possibly be right?

always be followed
by your shadow

OR

never see your
shadow at all?

On Valentine's Day, would you prefer to . . .

give your valentine
a card

OR

candy?

receive one special
valentine from
a best friend

OR

unsigned valentines from
every kid in your class?

have a secret
admirer

OR

be someone's
secret admirer?

For St. Patrick's Day, would you prefer to . . .

wear green every
day for a year

oR

have all your food dyed
green for a year?

eat corned beef
and cabbage every
day for a month

oR

go to school one day
in a leprechaun suit?

find a truly lucky
four-leaf clover

oR

discover the leprechaun's
pot of gold?

On Easter, would you prefer to . . .

spend the day eating
only chocolate eggs

oR

only jelly beans?

get a baby bunny

oR

a newborn chick?

decorate
100 Easter eggs

oR

search for
100 Easter eggs?

On Earth Day, would you prefer to . . .

organize a
tree-planting event

oR

a recycling drive?

give up paper napkins

oR

bottled water?

use a car that's
powered by air

oR

a lightbulb that
uses no electricity?

On Mother's Day, would you prefer to . . .

pamper your mom
with a manicure

OR

a massage?

give your mom
a beautiful
homemade card

OR

make her a
delicious meal?

tell your mom
a secret

OR

learn a secret
about her?

On Father's Day, would you prefer to . . .

make your dad
breakfast in bed

OR

take him out for
breakfast at his
favorite restaurant?

take over your dad's
duties inside the
house for the day

OR

do his jobs in
the yard for the day?

celebrate with a
pool party

OR

a family picnic?

On July 4th, would you prefer to . . .

enter a hot-dog
eating contest

OR

a potato-sack race?

watch a spectacular
fireworks show

OR

ride an upside-down
roller coaster?

dress up for the
day like Uncle Sam

OR

Lady Liberty?

For Halloween, would you prefer to . . .

carve
100 pumpkins

OR

bob for
100 apples?

wear your
Halloween costume
for a whole week

OR

not wear a
costume at all?

eat all your Halloween
candy on one night

OR

eat only one piece
a night until it's gone?

On Thanksgiving, would you prefer to . . .

prepare Thanksgiving
dinner for your family

OR

for people living at a
homeless shelter?

pluck feathers
from your own
Thanksgiving turkey

OR

peel 100 potatoes?

give thanks for
the things you have

OR

for the people
you know?

At Hanukkah, would you prefer to . . .

spin the dreidel
for 24 hours

OR

have the game end
after only one spin?

eat only sufganiyot
(jelly doughnuts)

OR

latkes (potato pancakes)?

celebrate Hanukkah
with just your family

OR

the entire
neighborhood?

For Christmas, would you prefer to . . .

take a ride on
a flying reindeer

OR

visit Santa's
workshop**?**

decorate your house
with tiny white lights

OR

with big, old-fashioned
colored lights**?**

make all the
presents you give

OR

buy them all
at the mall**?**

At Kwanzaa, would you prefer to . . .

only sing during
the celebration

OR

only dance**?**

make homemade
gifts for the family

OR

cook them a
homemade meal**?**

make a kinara
(candleholder)

OR

design a unity cup**?**

On New Year's Eve, would you prefer to . . .

ring in the new year
wearing your prettiest
party dress

OR

your pajamas**?**

stay in and celebrate
with your family

go out to a party
with your friends**?**

mark the stroke
of midnight by
banging pots and pans

by giving someone
a New Year's kiss**?**

Would you prefer to tell us your

"THIS OR THAT"

ideas in

A POSTCARD OR A LETTER?

Write to
This or That? Editor
American Girl
8400 Fairway Place
Middleton, WI 53562

(Sorry, but photos can't be returned. All comments
and suggestions received by American Girl may be
used without compensation or acknowledgment.)

Here are some other American Girl books you might like:

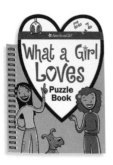

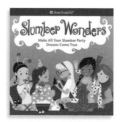

Each sold separately. Find more books online at americangirl.com.

Discover online games, quizzes, activities,
and more at **americangirl.com/play**